LATE INTERMEDIATE TO EARLY ADVANCED

Sunday Morning Blended Worship Companion

33 Selections of Praise Songs with Hymns

Arranged by Victor Labenske

The church today is often a complex musical landscape with both traditional sacred music and contemporary worship music playing complementary roles. *Sunday Morning Blended Worship Companion* presents 33 medleys that combine a hymn or traditional sacred song with a contemporary favorite. It includes arrangements at the late intermediate to early advanced levels for the church pianist who needs frequent material for preludes, offertories, postludes, and other service music. Arrangements are also appropriate for younger pianists who are looking for sacred music to augment their piano repertoire. My prayer is that pianists are able to use these arrangements to the glory of God while thinking about the lyrics and using playing as an act of worship.

Victor Labenske

Produced by Alfred Music
 Produced in U.S.A.
ISBN-10: 1-4706-2753-1
ISBN-13: 978-1-4706-2753-9

Cover Photo:
Happy people: © Shutterstock.com / Marijana Radonjic

(Approx. Performance Time – 3:45)

Amazing Grace
with
Amazing Grace (My Chains Are Gone)

20
f
dim.
rit.
24
a tempo
mp
cresc.
mf
mp rit.
p
29
a tempo
33
37

41
45
mp
49
53
cresc.
mf
57

62
cresc.
67
a tempo
rit.
mp
cresc.
72
mf
cresc.
77
rit. e dim.
mp
82
a tempo
p
rit.

(Approx. Performance Time – 3:00)

Be Thou My Vision
with
Center

Arr. Victor Labenske

cresc.
"Center"
Words and Music by Charlie Hall and Matt Redman
mf
p

43
mf
cresc.
47
f
mp
51
55
cresc.
59
mf

63
p
67
ped. simile
72
77
83
rit.

(Approx. Performance Time – 3:00)

Blessed Be Your Name
with
Blessed Be the Name

Driving rhythm (♩ = 132)

"Blessed Be Your Name"
Words and Music by Beth Redman and Matt Redman

Arr. Victor Labenske

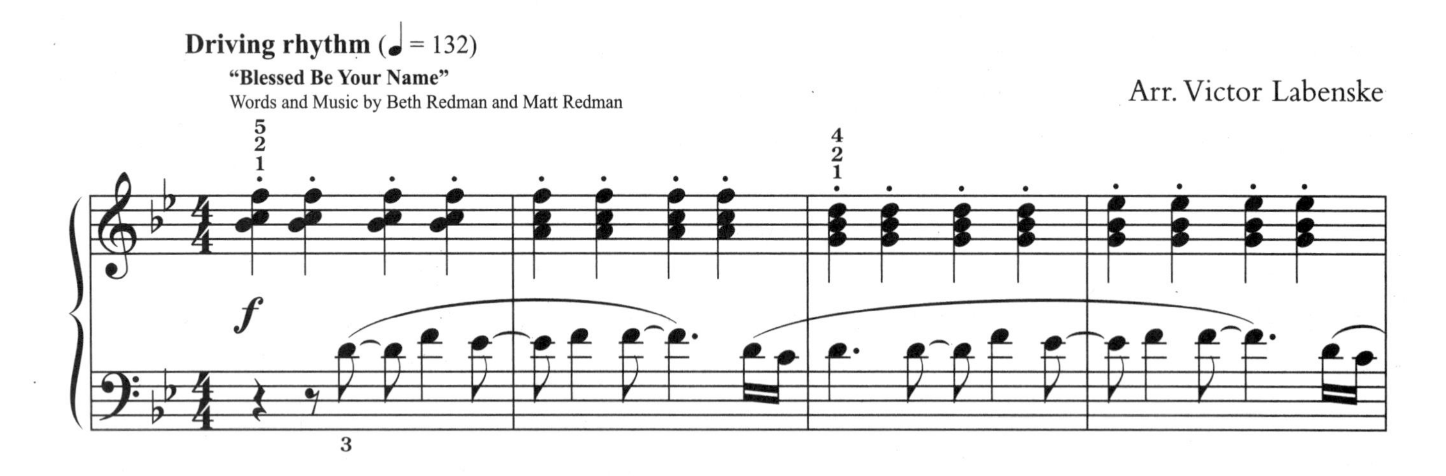

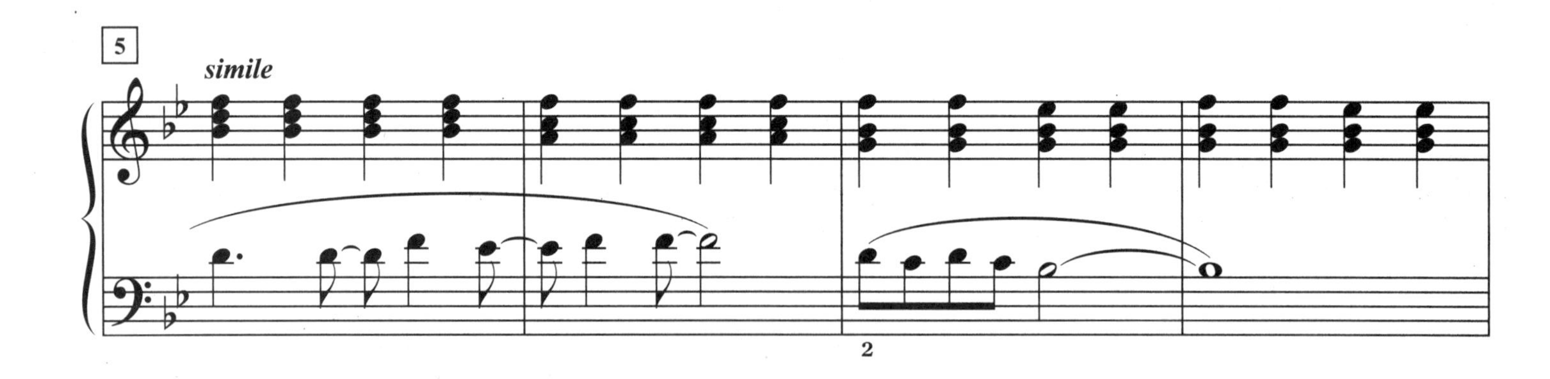

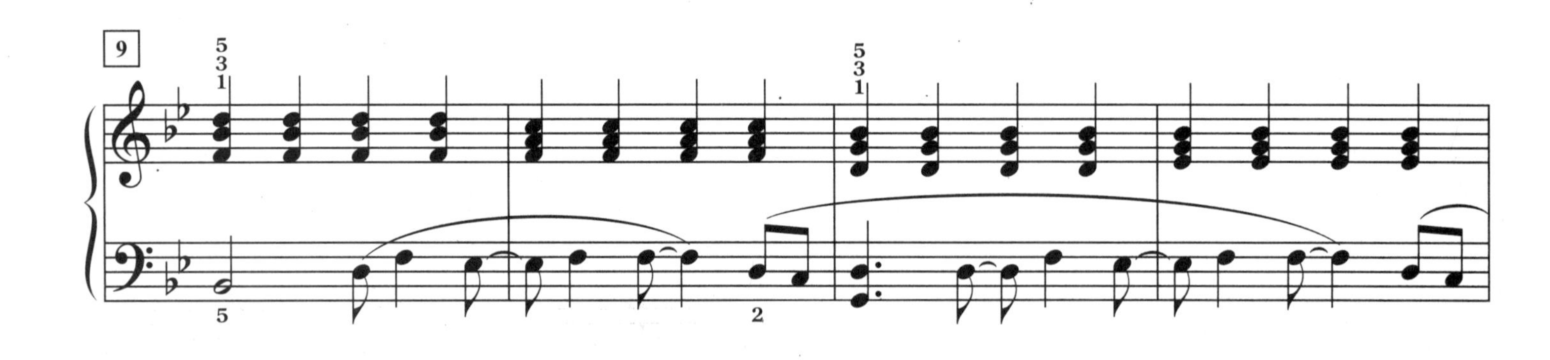

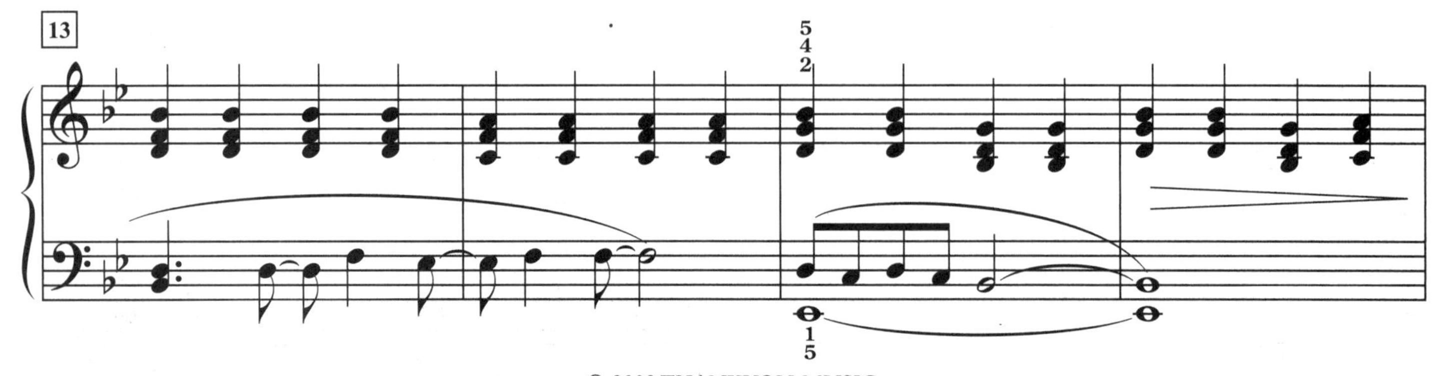

17
mf
simile
22
f
27
31
"Blessed Be the Name"
Traditional Christian Hymn
mf
35
ped. simile

40
a tempo
rit. e dim.
mp
45
mp
p
mp
p
mp
50
p
mp
p
mp
p
55
mp
p
mp
p
59
mp
cresc.

63
mf
67
cresc.
71
f
75
79
mp

83
mf
cresc.
87
a tempo
f
dim. e rit.
mp
91
mf
dim.
mp
95
a tempo
dim. e rit.
p
100
rit.

(Approx. Performance Time – 1:45)

Breathe On Me, Breath of God
with
Breathe

Arr. Victor Labenske

"Breathe"
Words and Music by Marie Barnett
Moving ahead (𝅗𝅥 = 72)
20
p accel.
mp
25
cresc.
30
mf
cresc.
35
f
40
mf
cresc.

44
f
48
dim.
rit.
52
a tempo
mp
dim.
56
p
rit.
60

(Approx. Performance Time – 2:15)

Cornerstone
with
The Solid Rock

Arr. Victor Labenske

17
f
dim.
mp

"The Solid Rock"
Music by William Bradbury
21
mf

24

28

32
f
36
mf
40
cresc.
f
44
mf
48
mp
rit. e dim.
p

(Approx. Performance Time – 2:53)

Everlasting God
with
A Mighty Fortress Is Our God

Arr. Victor Labenske

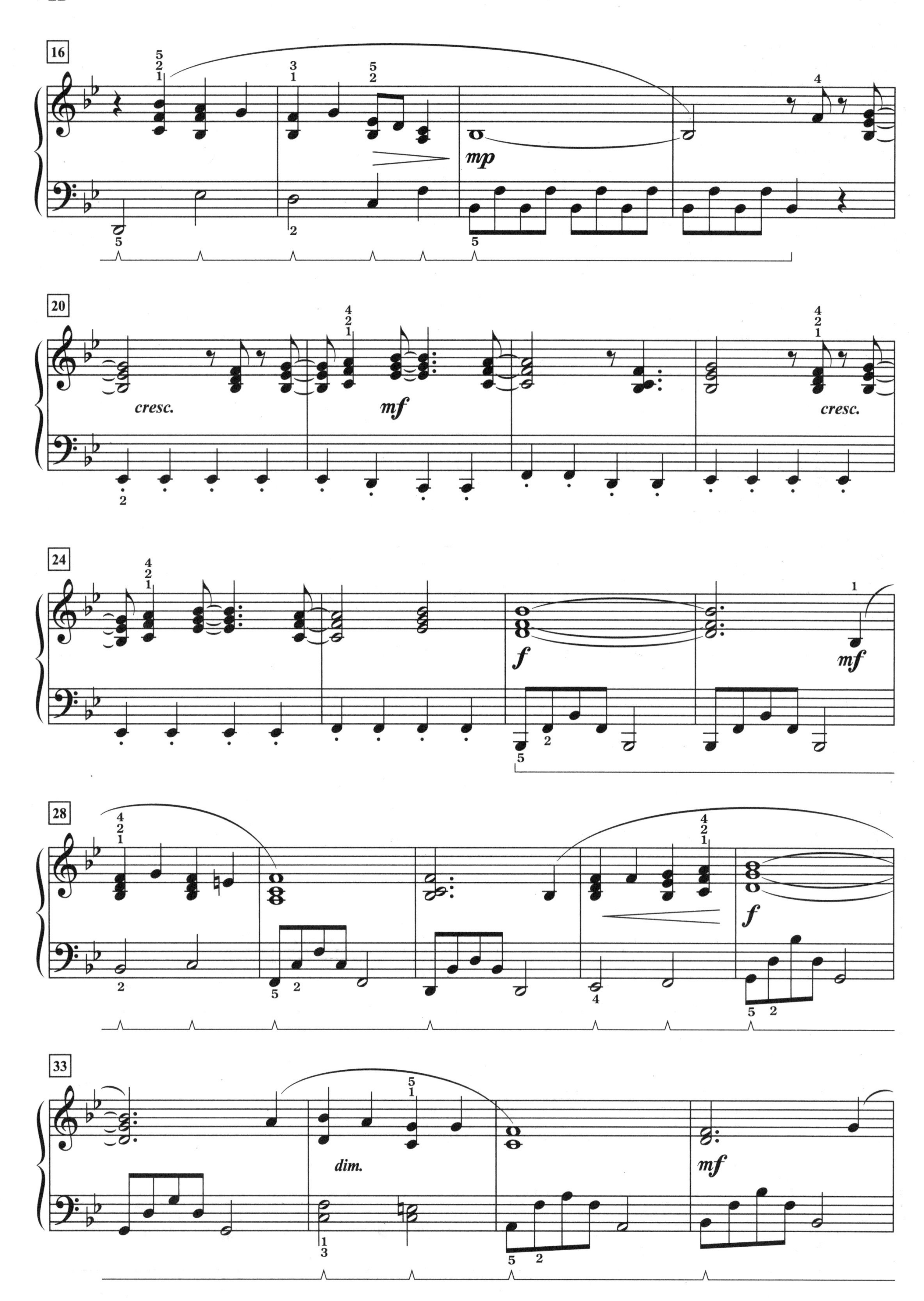
16
mp
20
cresc.
mf
cresc.
24
f
mf
28
f
33
dim.
mf

37
dim.
mp
41
cresc.
46
mf
50
cresc.
54
f
mf

58
cresc.
62
f
p
66
70
cresc.
mp
75
mf
cresc.

79
f
83
87
91
96
rit. e cresc.
ff

(Approx. Performance Time – 3:00)

Firm Foundation
with
The Church's One Foundation

Arr. Victor Labenske

mf
cresc.
"The Church's One Foundation"
Music by Samuel Wesley
f
mp

39
43
cresc.
47
a tempo
rit.
f
51
55

60
mf
64
p
melody
mf
69
74
79
a tempo
rit.
rit.
mp

(Approx. Performance Time – 2:30)

Forever Reign
with
Jesus Shall Reign

Arr. Victor Labenske

19
mf
23
27
"Jesus Shall Reign"
Music by John Hatton
mp
31
35
cresc. poco a poco

39
f
mf
43
mp
47
51
dim.
p
55
rit.

(Approx. Performance Time – 3:00)

God of Wonders
with
For the Beauty of the Earth

In awe (♩ = 72)

"God of Wonders"
Words and Music by Marc Byrd and Steve Hindalong

Arr. Victor Labenske

17
sub. p
accel.
cresc.
Somewhat faster (♩ = 88)
"For the Beauty of the Earth"
Music by Conrad Kocher
21
mp
mf
25
mp
cresc.
30
mf
cresc.
34
ten.
f
rit.

Tempo I (♩ = 72)
38
p
mp
42
cresc.
mf
46
ped. simile
50
mp
dim. poco a poco
55
rit.
pp

(Approx. Performance Time – 3:00)

Glorious Day (Living He Loved Me)
with
One Day

Arr. Victor Labenske

"One Day"
Music by Charles Marsh
cresc.
mf
dim.
p
cresc.
f

35
39
43
47
mf
ped. simile
51
f

54
8va
dim.
mp
58
ped. simile
62
66
p
70
rit.

(Approx. Performance Time – 2:30)

Glory to God Forever
with
To God Be the Glory

Arr. Victor Labenske

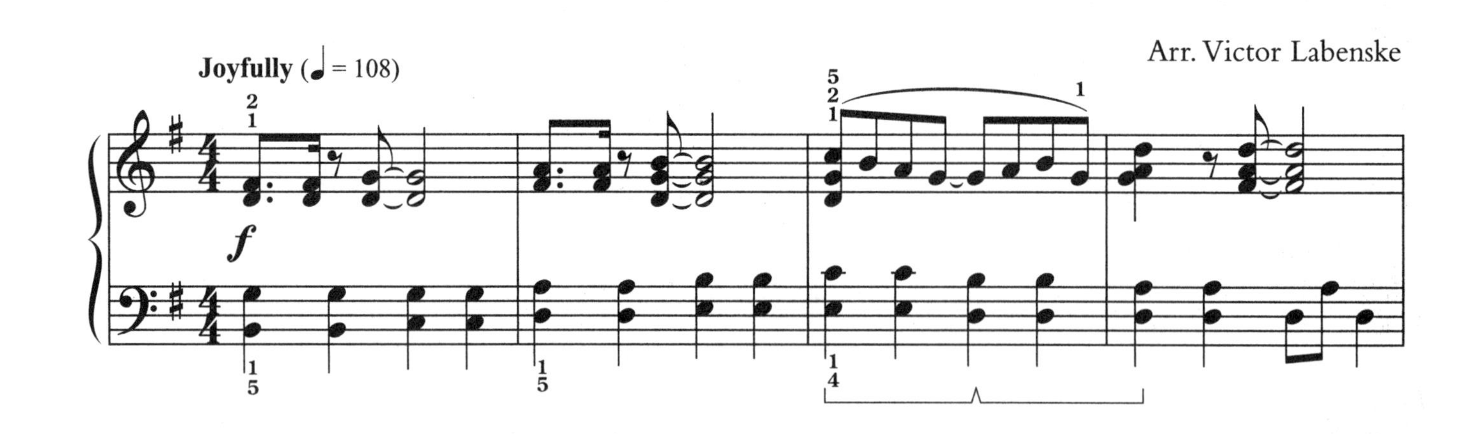

18
mf
23
cresc.
f
28
dim.
mp
32
mf
36

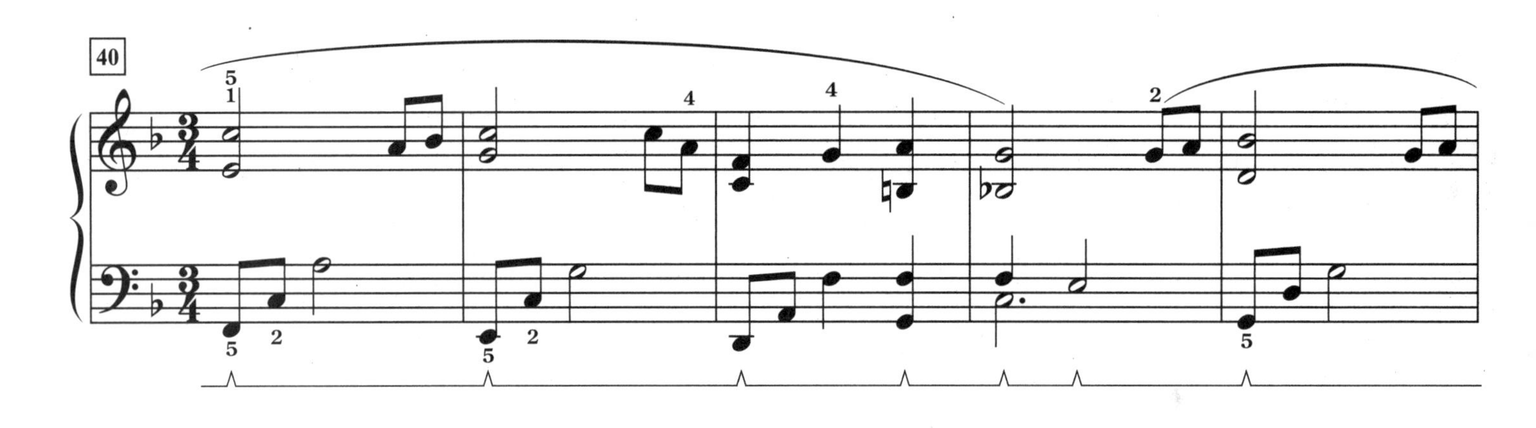
40

45
mp

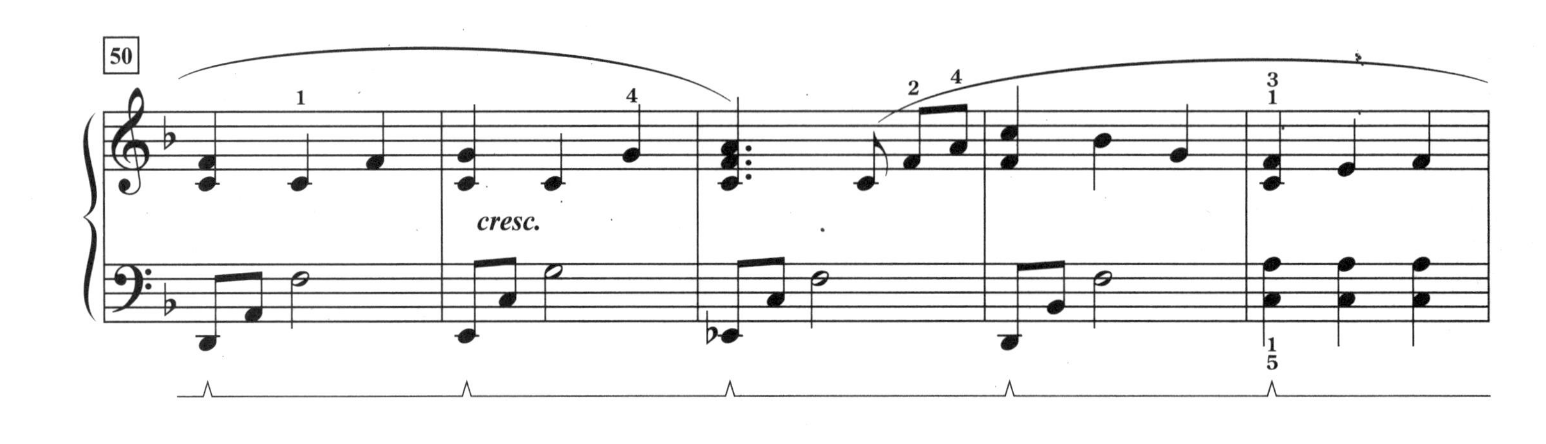
50
cresc.

55

59
f

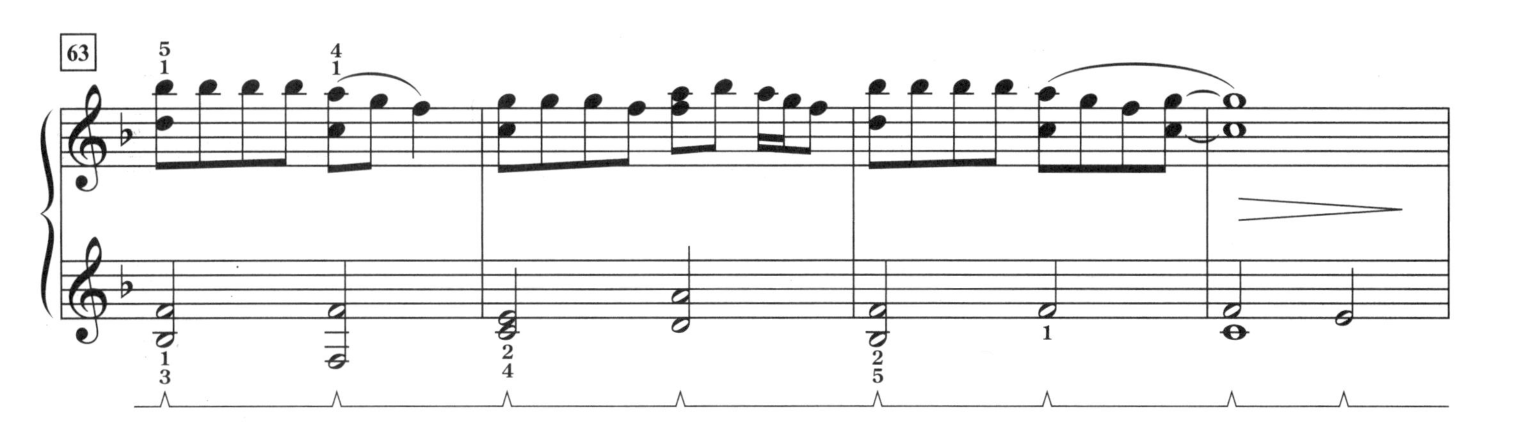
63

67
mp
rit.

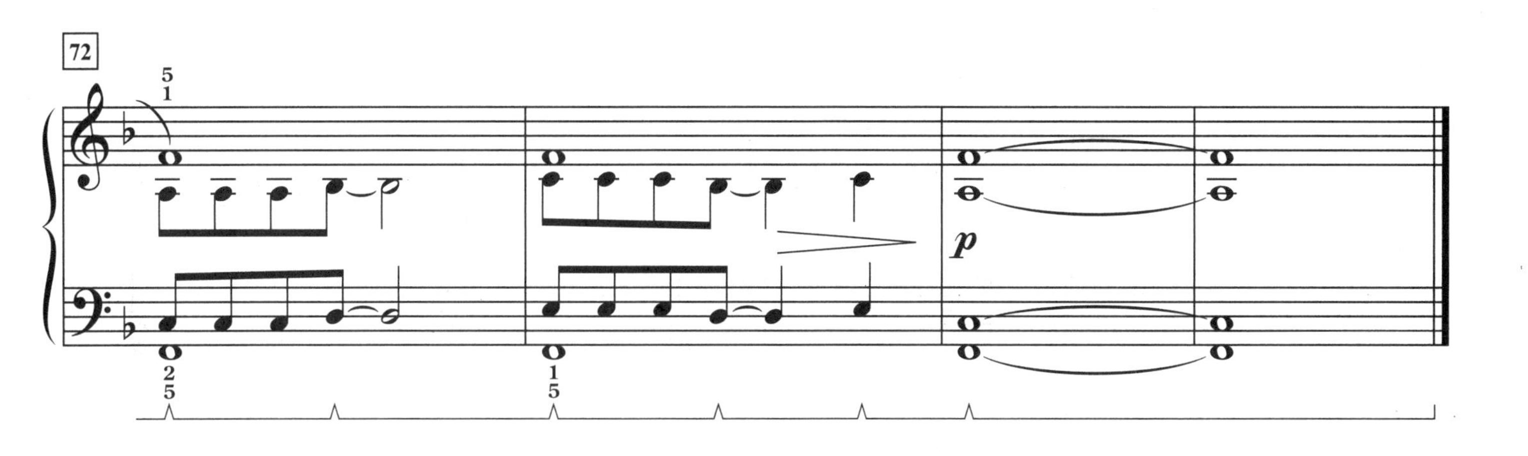
72
p

(Approx. Performance Time – 2:30)

The Heart of Worship
with
Nothing But the Blood

13
a tempo
mp
17
mf
rit. e dim.
21
a tempo
mp
25
cresc.
mf
28
p
cresc.

"Nothing But the Blood"
Words and Music by Robert Lowry
mp
ped. simile
p
mp
p
ped. simile
mp
p
mp
rit.
p

(Approx. Performance Time – 2:15)

Holy Is the Lord
with
Crown Him with Many Crowns

17
cresc.
ped. simile
21
mp
cresc. poco a poco
25
dim.
30
cresc.
35
mf
ped. simile

39
f
43
dim.
mf
p
mf
48
p
mp
ped. simile
53
58
a tempo
rit.
mp
p rit.

(Approx. Performance Time – 2:30)

Hosanna (Praise Is Rising)
with
Praise to the Lord, the Almighty

Arr. Victor Labenske

21
25
mf
29
mp
33
37
"Praise to the Lord, the Almighty"
Music by Joachim Neander
mf

43
mp
mf
49
p
mf
mf
54
ped. simile
mp cresc.
60
mf
65
ped. simile

f
mp
f
dim.
mp
cresc.
f cresc.
8va
ff

(Approx. Performance Time – 2:30)

How Great Thou Art
with
How Great Is Our God

Arr. Victor Labenske

16
cresc.
20
mf
mp
ped. simile
24
mf
cresc.
28
f
mf
32
f
a tempo
rit. e dim.
mp

"How Great Is Our God"

Words and Music by Jesse Reeves, Chris Tomlin, and Ed Cash

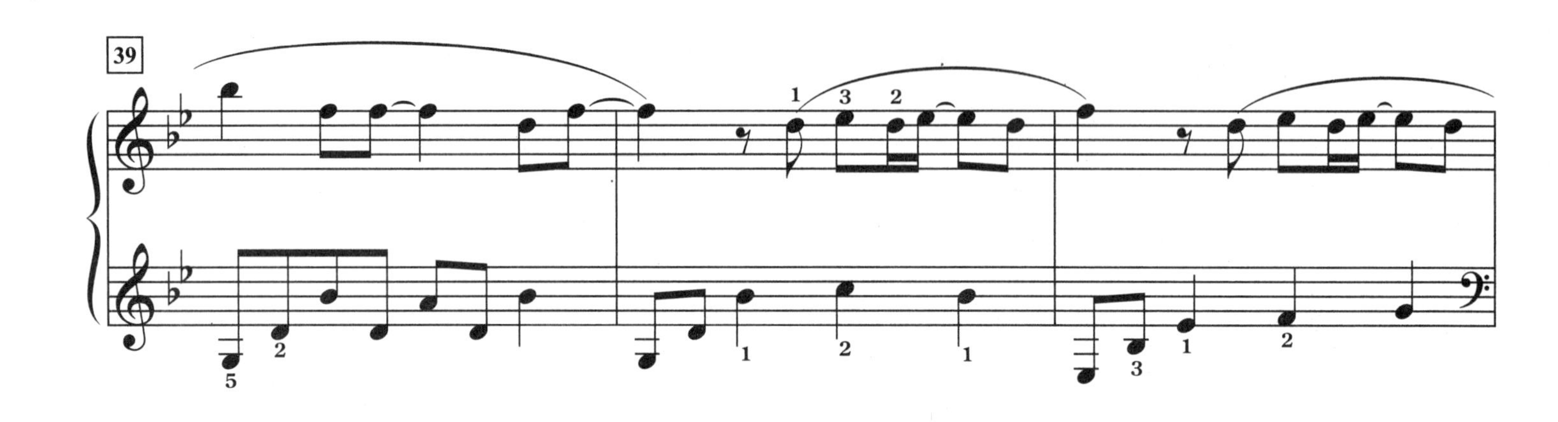

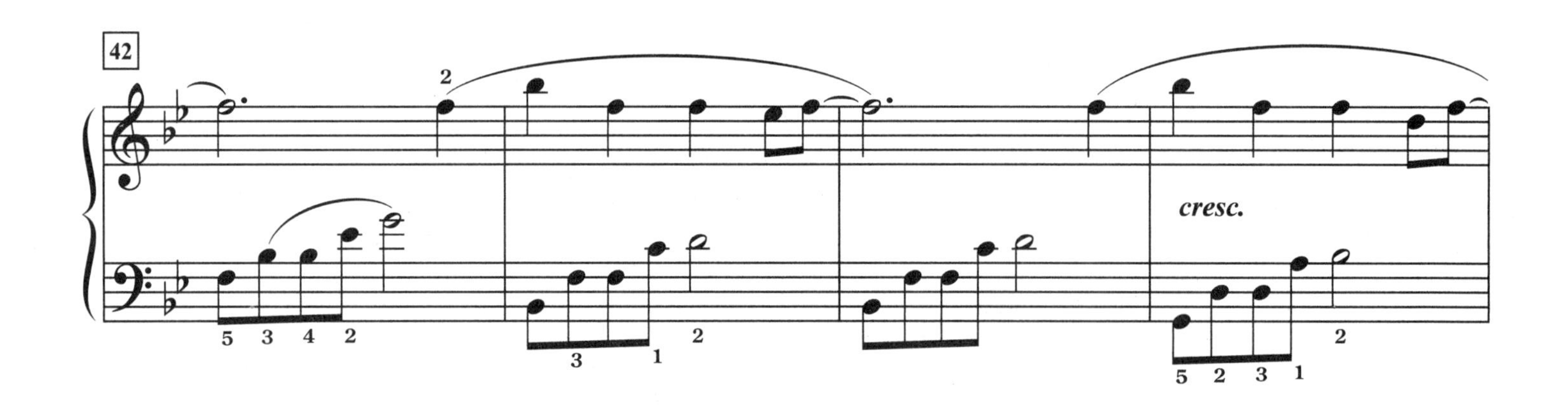

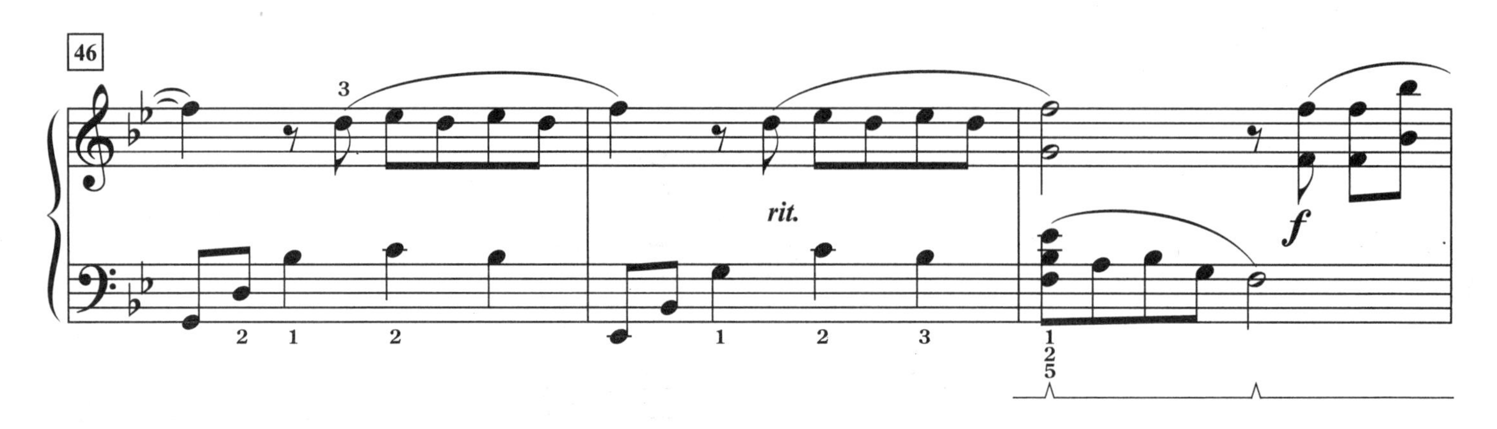

a tempo
49
52
mf
55
cresc.
f rit.
59
a tempo
rit.
ff

(Approx. Performance Time – 2:30)

How Can I Keep from Singing
with
Praise Him! Praise Him!

Arr. Victor Labenske

"Praise Him! Praise Him!"
Music by Chester Allen
21
26
31
36
41

46
51
56
61
66
mf
f
mf

71
cresc.
75
f
79
mf
84
cresc.
fp
cresc. poco a poco
88
f
ff

(Approx. Performance Time – 4:30)

Holy Spirit
with
Spirit of God, Descend Upon My Heart

Arr. Victor Labenske

21
25
"Spirit of God, Descend Upon My Heart"
Music by Frederick Atkinson
mf
29
33
cresc.
37
f
dim.
rit.

40
a tempo
pp
p
mp
45
ped. simile
50
cresc.
54
mf
58

62
cresc.
66
f
rit. e dim.
70
a tempo
mp
73
p
mp
77
p

81
8va
pp
p
85
8va
pp
p
89
8va
pp
p
93
97
8va
rit. e dim.
pp

(Approx. Performance Time – 2:45)

I Exalt Thee
with
I Surrender All

Arr. Victor Labenske

"I Surrender All"
Music by Winfield Weeden
rit.
a tempo

37
ten.
p
sub. p
41
46
pp
51
56
p
rit.

(Approx. Performance Time – 3:30)

I Will Rise
with
My Savior First of All

Arr. Victor Labenske

21
25
29
rit. e dim.
Tempo rubato (♩ = ca. 84)
"My Savior First of All"
Music by John R. Sweeney
33
mp
38

42
46
mf
mp rit.
accel.
Moving forward (♩ = 96)
50
54
mf
cresc.
58
f
dim.

pp
ped. simile
p rit.
a tempo
8va
rit. e dim.
pp

(Approx. Performance Time – 4:30)

I NEED THEE EVERY HOUR
WITH
LORD, I NEED YOU

Arr. Victor Labenske

16
dim.
20
mp
p
"Lord, I Need You"
Words and Music by Christy Nockels, Daniel Carson,
Jesse Reeves, Kristian Stanfill, and Matt Maher
24
mp
ten.
28
32
mf

8va
8va
ped. simile

54
8va
p
mp
58
8va
p
62
mp
cresc.
66
mf
f
dim.
70
p
mp

74
p
mp
78
mf
82
85
dim.
rit.
89
a tempo
p
rit.

(Approx. Performance Time – 4:00)

It Is Well
with
It Is Well with My Soul

14
mf
17
dim.
p
20
"It Is Well with My Soul"
Music by Philip Bliss
24
mp
26

28
30
32
mf
cresc.
35
f
38
mp
f

41
ped. simile
44
dim.
47
mp
50
dim.
p
mp
p
53
mp
p
mp

56
mf
dim.
59
8va
p
pp
62
66
70
rit.

(Approx. Performance Time – 3:15)

Jesus Paid It All
with
Jesus Paid It All (Oh Praise the One)

Arr. Victor Labenske

a tempo
rit.
mp
"Jesus Paid It All (Oh Praise the One)"
Words and Music by Alex Nifong
a tempo
pp
mp
ped. simile
mf
cresc.

42
46
a tempo
rit.
50
mf
rit.
a tempo
mp
54
cresc.
mf
ped. simile
58
cresc.
f

62
rit.
66
a tempo
mp
rit.
a tempo
70
ped. simile
75
8va
dim.
p
80
rit.
pp
8va

(Approx. Performance Time – 3:30)

My Faith Has Found a Resting Place
with
Enough

Arr. Victor Labenske

16
cresc.
20
mf
dim.
mp
24
28
33
ped. simile

37
mf
mp
cresc.
41
f
45
mp
49
cresc.
ped. simile
53
mf

56
f
59
dim.
mp
63
a tempo
rit.
p
67
72
rit.

(Approx. Performance Time – 3:00)

No, Not One
with
No, Not One!

Arr. Victor Labenske

21
f
25
29
mf
33
"No, Not One!"
Music by George Hugg
ped. simile
37

41
45
mp
49
mf
53
57
cresc.
f

61
ped. simile
65
dim.
mf
69
p
73
77
rit.
RH over

(Approx. Performance Time – 2:30)

O Praise Him, All This for a King
with
Rejoice, the Lord Is King

Arr. Victor Labenske

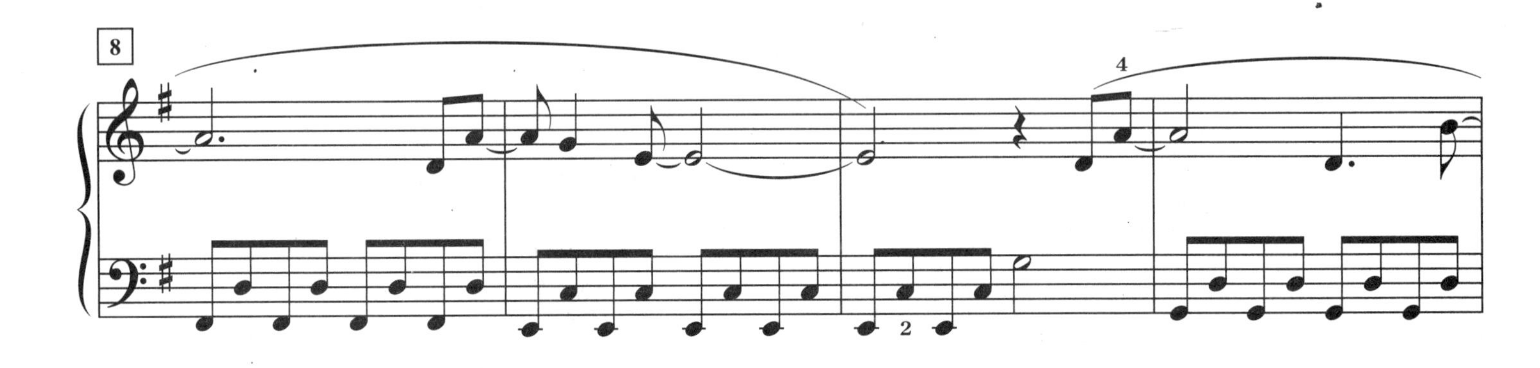

16
4
cresc.
3
19
1
4
mf
3
5
3
23
1
4
1
27
1
cresc.
31
1
1
f
2
5
2
5
5
2

34
38
"Rejoice, the Lord Is King"
Music by John Darwall
mp
42
cresc.
46
f
mf
50
sub. p
cresc.
f

53
mf
57
61
mp
65
dim.
69
8va
rit.
p

(Approx. Performance Time – 2:30)

Mighty to Save
with
Arise, My Soul, Arise

Arr. Victor Labenske

"Arise, My Soul, Arise"
Music by Lewis Edson
mf
f
mf

31
mp
35
cresc.
39
mf
mp
43
p
47
cresc.
mp rit. e dim.
p

(Approx. Performance Time – 2:30)

Oceans (Where Feet May Fail)
with
'Tis So Sweet to Trust in Jesus

Arr. Victor Labenske

mp
rit. e dim.
a tempo
p
mp
cresc.
mf
mp
mf
mp

mf
dim.
p
cresc.
mp
8va
pp
rit.

(Approx. Performance Time – 3:45)

One Thing Remains (Your Love Never Fails)
with
Jesus Never Fails

Arr. Victor Labenske

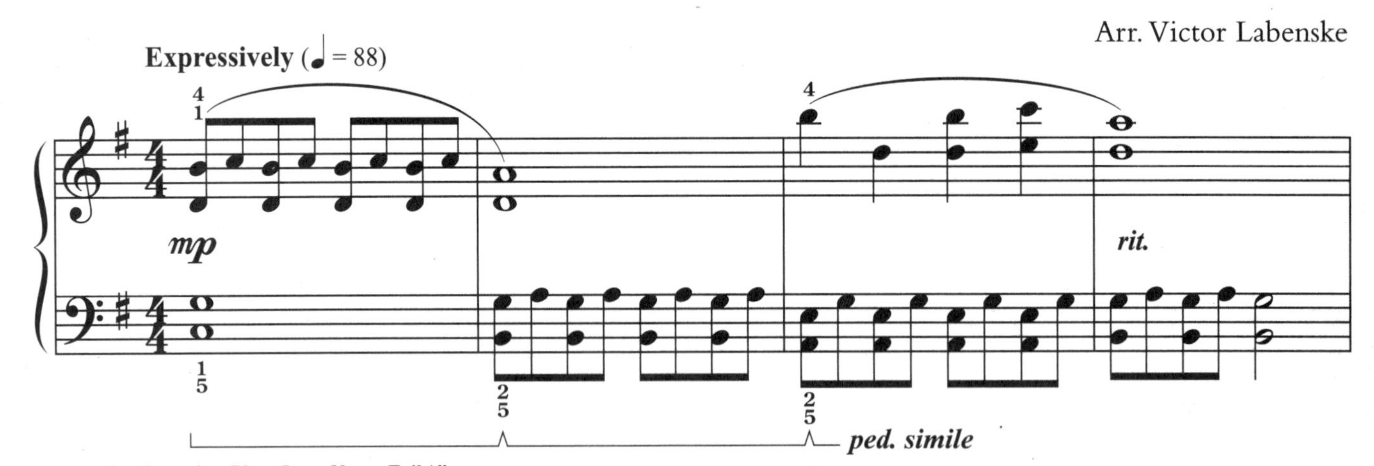

"One Thing Remains (Your Love Never Fails)"
Words and Music by Jeremy Riddle, Brian Johnson, and Christa Black

17
dim.
mp
21
cresc.
mf
dim.
25
mp
p
29
pp
mp
33
rit.

37
a tempo
mp
mp
40
mp
cresc.
rit.
43
a tempo
mf
rit. e dim.
a tempo
p
47
cresc.
ped. simile
mp
50
cresc.

53
mf
cresc.
57
f
60
mp
63
cresc.
ped. simile
67
f

70
sub. p
73
rit.
a tempo
76
mf
f
79
ff
82
rit.

(Approx. Performance Time – 2:00)

Our God
with
How Firm a Foundation

16
20
24
ped. simile
28
32

36
mp
40
mf
mp
44
mf
48
cresc.
52
f
ff

(Approx. Performance Time – 2:45)

Revelation Song
with
Holy, Holy, Holy

Arr. Victor Labenske

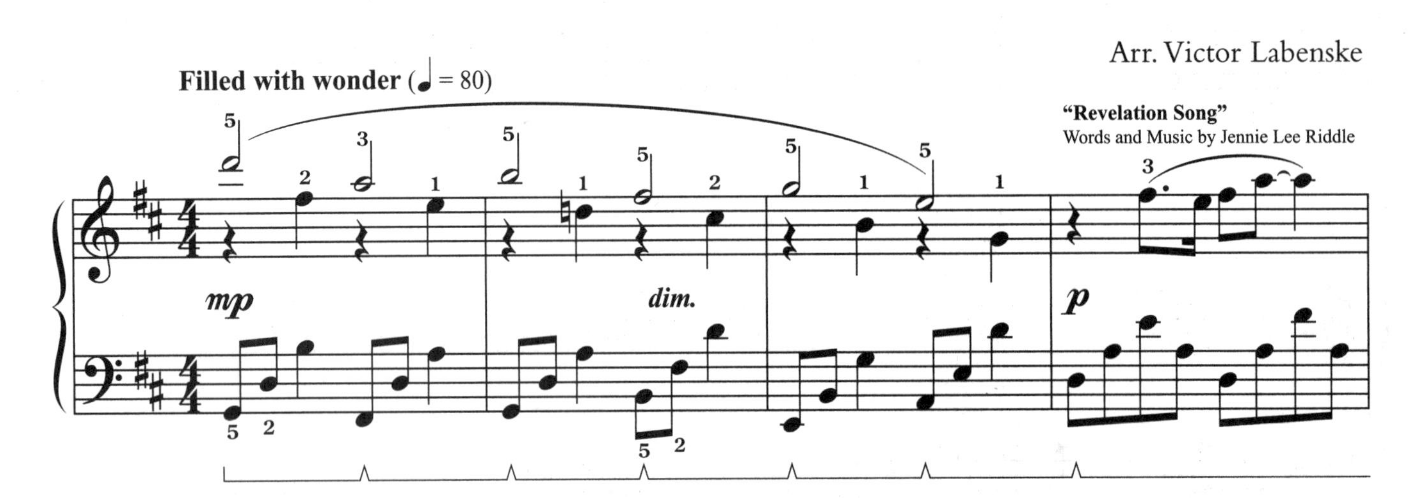

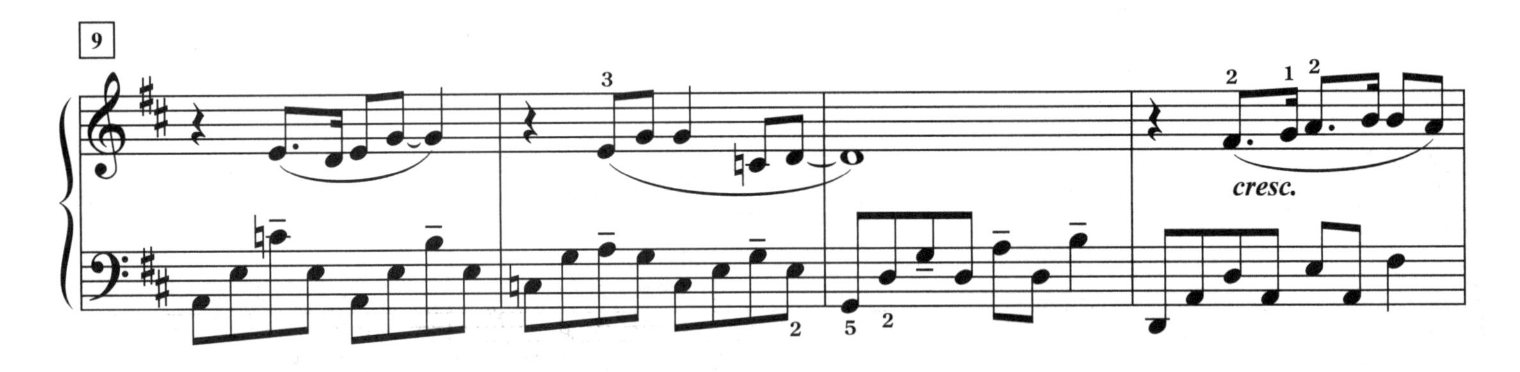

17
cresc.
f
dim.
21
"Holy, Holy, Holy"
Music by John Bacchus Dykes (Nicaea)
mp
25
p
cresc.
29
mf
33
mp
cresc.

37
a tempo
mf
p
mp
rit.
41
pp
calmly
mp
RH over
45
49
53
rit.

(Approx. Performance Time – 2:30)

When Morning Gilds the Skies
with
10,000 Reasons (Bless the Lord)

Arr. Victor Labenske

"10,000 Reasons (Bless the Lord)"
Words and Music by Matt Redman and Jonas Myrin

40
cresc. poco a poco
ped. simile
44
f
48
52
ff
rit.
a tempo
mp
cresc.
56
f
rit. e cresc.
ff

(Approx. Performance Time – 3:00)

When I Survey the Wondrous Cross
with
The Wonderful Cross

17
22
"The Wonderful Cross"
Words and Music by Chris Tomlin, J. D. Walt, and Jesse Reeves
26
mf
30
34

38
42
sub. p
46
rit.
50
a tempo
54

58
63
68
mp
72
rit. e dim.
76
a tempo
p
rit.

(Approx. Performance Time – 3:45)

Your Grace Finds Me
with
Grace Greater Than Our Sin

Arr. Victor Labenske

13
p
mp
p
16
mp
cresc.
19
mf
22
25

28
f
Somewhat faster (♩ = 112)
"Grace Greater Than Our Sin"
Music by Daniel Towner
31
accel.
sub. p
cresc.
ped. simile
35
mp
cresc.
40
mf
cresc.
44
f
dim.
mp

A little slower (♩ = 100)
49
rit. e dim.
pp
54
59
64
rit.
Tempo I (♩ = 80)
68

72
p
cresc.
mp
ped. simile
75
cresc.
mf
cresc.
78
f
dim.
82
mp
dim.
86
8va
p
rit. e dim.
pp